# Creating Published Diamonds

## Books by Deb Donnell

Critiquing Writing Diamonds

Christchurch Comparison 2015 Edition

Christchurch, NZ: Comparing 2014 to Pre-Earthquake

Responders: The New Zealand Volunteer Response Teams
Christchurch Earthquake Deployments (with Pete Seager)

Café Reflections Christchurch City

Trails to Treasure

**Writing Diamonds**

TRANSFORMING WRITING ROCKS INTO PUBLISHED DIAMONDS

# Creating
# Published Diamonds

Introducing
**Deb Donnell's**
Diamond Publishing System™

Keswin Publishing

Published by

Keswin Publishing Ltd
P O Box 21-138, Edgeware
Christchurch 8143, New Zealand
KeswinPublishing.com

Creating Published Diamonds
Edition ISBNs
PDF: 978-0-9582780-8-9
Print: 978-0-9582780-9-6
eBook: 978-0-985780-0-3

The *Diamond Publishing System*™ is fully licensed
to Writing Diamonds Ltd, and The Diamond
Publishing Training Centre. For more
information or to join us please
visit WritingDiamonds.com

A catalogue of this book is available from
the National Library of New Zealand

*'Before a diamond shows its brilliancy and prismatic colors it has to stand a good deal of cutting and smoothing.'*

*Author Unknown*

# Contents

# Acknowledgements

Natural diamonds form in extreme pressure and high temperature situations. Over the years I've been blessed with many such situations in which to form my writing diamonds. I have also been fortunate to have people help me in a variety of roles as I have worked at creating, mining, cutting, and polishing the *Diamond Publishing System™*.

I want to acknowledge some of these brilliant diamonds in my life:

The foundation members of the Diamond Publishing Training Centre who bravely road tested the training material: Addie Bissey, Arne Bush, Corinne Floyd, Greg Gust, Heather Hansen, Marshall Joyce (1932-2014) Claire Newell, Kristie Newland, Lanette Passarelli, Tom Renfro, Dennis Roberts (1948-2015), Barb Schacher, Carol Smith, Helen Sonobe, Nicole Thomas, Felicia Waren, Tania Wilder, and Bob Young. Thank you for having faith in me, especially when I was only a few steps ahead of you on some topics.

In recent years I have been very fortunate to have Ivan Hatherley as my publishing mentor. He has a very deep and rich diamond mine of KESWIN about the publishing industry. Having him on my team has reaffirmed my own knowledge, and helped me move forward and achieve my dream of owning a successful publishing company. Thank you, Ivan, for sharing your publishing diamonds with me.

Thank you, Pete Seager, co-author of Responders. You encouraged me to give *The Diamond Publishing System*™ a tough road test in 2012 and 2013 with the Christchurch Earthquake titles. Your belief in my abilities helped me to find many of the diamonds I lost in the earthquake rubble.

My parents, Ngaio and Richard Donnell, who have been there for me all my life, and my sisters, brother-in-laws, nieces and nephews, aunts, uncles and cousins. Thank you for your support over the years.

My partner, Eric Donn, who understands my need to own and operate a business. Thank you for riding the business roller coaster with me. Thank you for not letting me give up and get a 'real job', especially on the days when finding profitable writing diamonds seems overwhelmingly impossible.

# Disclaimer

This book is designed to provide information on writing and publishing. It is sold with the understanding that neither the author nor the publisher is engaged in rendering legal, accounting or other professional services. If legal or other expert assistance is required, the services of an appropriate professional should be sought.

It is not the purpose of this book to be an exhaustive and complete presentation on writing and publishing. Every effort has been made to make the information presented here as complete and accurate as possible. However, there may be mistakes, both typographical and in content. Therefore this text should be used only as a general guide and not as the ultimate source of writing and publishing. Furthermore, this book contains information on writing and publishing that is current only up to the publication date.

Every effort has been made to trace and acknowledge copyright material; should any infringement have occurred accidentally, the author tenders her apologies.

The purpose of this book is to educate and entertain. The author and publisher shall have neither liability or responsibility to any person or entity with respect to any loss or damage alleged to have been caused, directly or indirectly, by the information, ideas, opinions or other content in this book.

**If you do not agree to these terms, you should return this book immediately for full refund, or unsubscribe from any list you may have joined to receive a complimentary copy.**

## Welcome

Hi, I'm Deb Donnell. I was born into, and have been involved for most of my life with New Zealand's jewellery industry. In 2011 I graduated with the Gemological Institute of America's (GIA) Diamonds & Diamond Grading Diploma. I am fascinated by diamonds. They are beautiful gemstones, each with a story that began more than 3 billions years ago.

The stones we see today formed about 100 kilometres below the continental crust in the diamond stability field — an area of the earth's mantle that has the right temperature and pressure environment for carbon to become crystallised rather than turn into graphite.

Then these rough diamond crystals are gathered up by volcanic rock (kimberlite), and transported to the earth's surface at speeds of around 300 kilometres per hour. After this violent arrival they are scattered around the craters of the kimberlite pipes, or washed down into rivers which deliver them to a resting place in the ocean.

Finding diamonds is a long and expensive process. Explorers and their investors must be patient, and persist against all odds to find viable diamond pipes. Only about one in 250 deposits discovered are determined to be economic after lengthy feasibility studies.

Then it will take several years for the mine to be given permits and constructed. The financial investment in the whole process is hundreds of millions of dollars.

Diamonds are then mined, graded, cut, polished and set into jewellery. Each gem-quality diamond that we see for sale in jewellery stores has gone through a long labour intensive process. To give you an idea of how labour intensive — a tonne of rubble needs to be shifted and sifted to produce a round brilliant cut half carat diamond.

---

## How big is a half carat diamond?

*It is 5.2 mm in diameter, and weighs one tenth of a gram (100 milligrams). As a comparison, it is the same average weight of a coffee bean.*

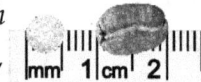

*Diamonds were originally weighed against carob seeds, which weigh, on average, 200 milligrams. So a 1.00 carat diamond equals the weight of one carob seed.*

---

A published book goes through a similar process of creation, discovery, feasibility testing, mining, grading, manufacturing and marketing.

Fortunately it doesn't cost hundreds of millions of dollars to produce a book! However a best selling book does require a significant investment of time and finances on behalf of the author and publisher. Some books are years in the making, and even more years trying to convince a publishing house to acquire the manuscript. Self-publishing can short-cut the time to market, and skilled authors can also reduce production costs significantly.

My fascination with writing and publishing began at the age of ten, when I self-published my first book. I enjoyed it so much, I decided that when I grew up, I would become a writer and publisher. However, the career advice I received from well-meaning loved ones put me on a much safer path into a full-time job in the banking industry (with part-time involvement in my parents' jewellery business).

I travelled to the UK in my early twenties, and got my dream job working in a publishing house in Bath. I was in heaven.

However, my work visa in the UK was only for two years. When I returned to New Zealand there were no jobs in publishing, so I went back to working full-time in the bank, and helping my father with jewellery valuations part-time. I left banking in 1999 to study at university, and continued working part-time in the jewellery business.

I founded the *Diamond Publishing System*™ in 2003. I wanted to develop a simple and affordable process that allowed writers to self-publish and network with other writers. This was before the Internet and technology evolved into what we know today. It's amazing how much has changed in such a short time.

It made perfect sense to blend the publishing and diamond journeys together. I began to test my system with the members of my writing group. In 2008 I co-founded an online training site and continued testing and refining it with the help of our members.

When I finished studying at university in 2005, I increased my hours working in the jewellery business to full-time. I also set up Keswin Publishing Ltd, and started to self-publish. It was a part-time venture at first. After we lost the jewellery store premises in the 2011 Christchurch Earthquake, I decided it was time to get serious about my publishing dream.

My focus is now to help people to write and publish their diamond-quality non-fiction books. I believe that books are such a valuable way to create legacies, share knowledge, educate others, and more. I prefer to focus on non-fiction books, although I have studied and written novels in several fiction genres as well.

Non-fiction books are the perfect marketing tool for any expert, leader or business person wanting to establish their credibility and authority in their community. They can be sold as separate products, used as up-sells, bonuses or even promotional giveaways.

Now that I've given you a brief introduction to my story, it's time to look more closely at the shared journey of diamonds and publishing.

But before we do, let me share with you my primary mission, which is to help one million people release the books trapped inside of them.

So, if this book helps you do this, please let me know. My contact details are on the last page of this book.

*Helping you transform your writing rocks into published diamonds.*

**Deb Donnell**

*Author, Publisher, Mentor*
*GIA Diamonds Graduate*
*Professional Editing & Proofreading Certificate*
*(Sackville Academy)*

# Introducing
# The Diamond Publishing System™

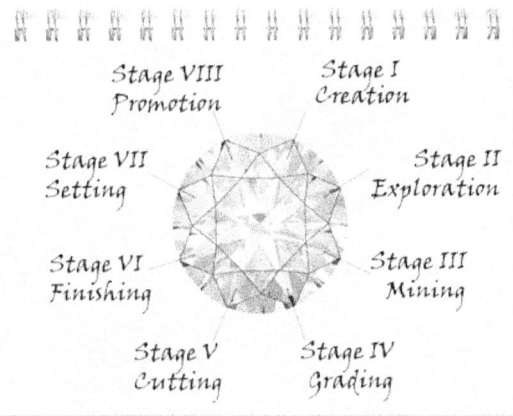

Stage VIII
Promotion

Stage I
Creation

Stage VII
Setting

Stage II
Exploration

Stage VI
Finishing

Stage III
Mining

Stage V
Cutting

Stage IV
Grading

The *Diamond Publishing System*™ is based on the journey of natural diamonds and applied to the writing, editing, production and promotion of books and other written projects.

The diamond analogy used in the *Diamond Publishing System*™ is a reference to the gems of ideas, knowledge, information and stories that you have to share with others. To avoid confusion, we will differentiate between them as 'real, crystallised carbon or natural diamonds', versus 'your intangible, writing or published diamonds'.

If you do find anywhere that we haven't made clear which diamonds (real or intangible) we are referring to, please let us know so we can update this book. You can do this by emailing us at the address on the last page of this book.

The *Diamond Publishing System*™ is an eight step process that helps you take your ideas and turn them into marketable publications. Or, more simply, it *transforms your writing rocks into published diamonds*.

This book is an overview of the *Diamond Publishing System*™. This overview may be enough information for some people interested in the self-publishing process. If you require a deeper understanding, Writing Diamonds provides training manuals, online learning, group workshops and private mentoring. You will find more about these options at the end of this book.

In the meantime, please get ready to create some rough writing diamonds and transform them into published gemstones.

*'When we long for life without difficulties,*
*remind us that oaks grow strong in contrary winds*
*and diamonds are made under pressure.'*

*Peter Marshall*
*(American TV game show host, b.1927)*

# Diamond Creator

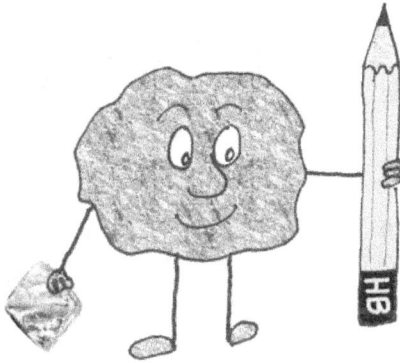

*Natural diamonds are created in the diamond stability field in the earth's mantle. Writing diamonds are created from internal response to external stimuli. Stage I looks at how you create your intangible diamonds, and transport them into physical form.*

## *Stage I: Creation (Formation)*

Diamonds and writing are more closely related than people realise. The word graphite comes from the Greek word γράφειν (graphein) which means 'to write or draw'.

The core of a pencil is made of non-toxic graphite, so when you are writing with a pencil, you are writing with an allotrope of carbon.

Diamonds are also an allotrope of carbon. The differences in the final composition of the carbon depends on the physical conditions in the earth's mantle during creation.

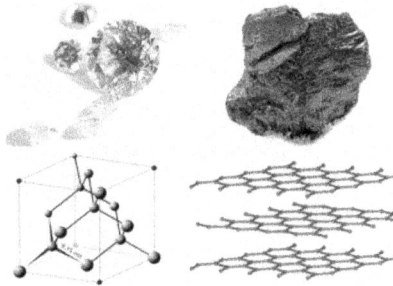

Diamond and graphite are allotropes of carbon, with different compositions. Above are samples of each with their respective structures.

You could say that the difference between your writing rocks and your rough writing diamonds will depend on the conditions during their formation.

Like natural diamonds, writing diamonds are created, not made. They form deep in your psyche during the course of your life. Your rough writing diamonds are created under extreme heat and pressure from external and internal forces that influence your thoughts, behaviour and personality.

## Formation

Think of your rough writing diamonds as any of the following:

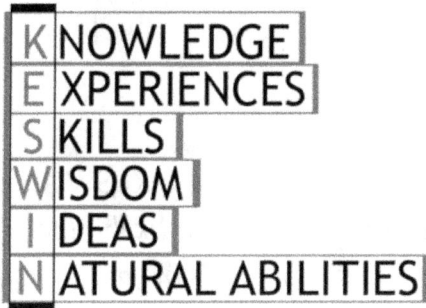

```
K NOWLEDGE
E XPERIENCES
S KILLS
W ISDOM
I DEAS
N ATURAL ABILITIES
```

These words form the anagram, KESWIN.

Remember this anagram, as we will make reference to it again.

You may also have noticed that this anagram is the same as the name of my publishing company, Keswin Publishing Ltd.

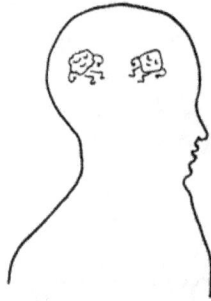

*Have you developed any valuable KESWIN throughout your lifetime? If so, then it is very likely that you have been creating rough writing diamonds in your subconscious.*

*If you feel it is time to wake them up and transport them into physical form, then read on.*

## Emplacement

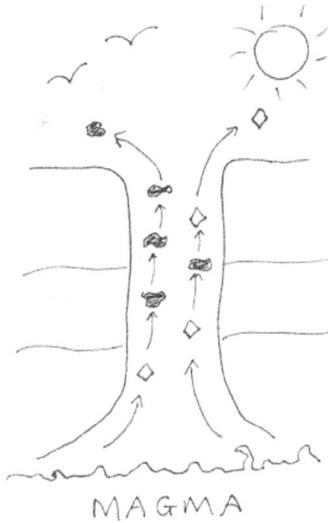

MAGMA

Natural diamonds are transported to the earth's surface by kimberlite, which is a volcanic rock. The kimberlite originates lower in the earth's mantle than the diamond stability field. As it passes through the field, it collects the diamonds on its way to the earth's surface.

When a volcano erupts, the lava it ejects can flow over a large area (for tens of kilometers). When the lava cools, it becomes hardened rock.

Not all volocanoes are kimberlite pipes, and not all kimberlite pipes are diamond bearing. It has taken explorers centuries to discover the diamond rich areas on Earth, with the most recent being discovered in the Canadian Arctic Circle in 1991.

The process of transporting your writing diamonds into physical form isn't quite as violent as a volcanic eruption (at least we hope not!). But it does produce significantly more rocks than diamonds.

This fact is often one overlooked by novice writers. They unrealistically expect to produce polished writing diamond after polished writing diamond every time they sit down to write.

When the first attempt isn't perfect, a novice writer runs the risk of giving up. It is important to be gentle with yourself when you write. You need to accept that you are in the early stages of skill development, and it will take a lot of practice and constructive feedback to become a master.

This is why the first stage of the *Diamond Publishing System*™ is so important. It will help you unlearn any bad habits you've been taught about writing, remove the unrealistic expectations you have about your first drafts, and help you to address and overcome any blocks that prevent you from achieving your goals.

## Writer's Block

*I can't disturb
the cat*

*Therefore I must
have Writer's Block*

*Medical Definition of writer's block:
A psychological inhibition preventing a writer from proceeding with a piece of writing.
—Merriam-Webster Medical Dictionary*

So, overcoming writer's block is not as simple as removing a physical object from your keyboard or notepad. However, most people can overcome writer's block by learning one or two proven writing techniques, which we'll teach you shortly.

The danger of writer's block is that people will use it as an excuse to give up their writing dream. It nearly stopped me in my mid twenties, when I would tell people that I wanted to write a book, but hadn't started because I had nothing to write about. The reality was I had low self-confidence and believed I had nothing of value to share.

Fortunately I discovered some mentors who helped me overcome my inhibitions.

*Have you ever experienced writer's block?*

Signs of this infliction are:

- When handwriting, you may stare at a blank page for long periods of time, or will have several crumpled up sheets of paper scattered around you.

- When working on a computer, the open file page will be blank, or you will be surfing the Internet in the guise of needing to do more research.

## What Causes Writer's Block?

The cause is usually one of two reasons:

1. Well meaning teachers or loved ones have judged your work harshly in the past, so you have lost confidence in your writing abilities.

2. You have an unrealistic expectation about the quality of writing you will produce first time.

To overcome writer's block, learn the Writing Practice techniques we're about to show you, and commit to writing every day in order to develop your skills.

*Please don't let writer's block stop you from getting started, or cause you to give up after a few attempts.*

## Writing Practice

The best way to transport your writing rocks and rough diamonds into physical form is through using first thought processes, such as journalling, word or picture prompts, mind mapping or brainstorming.

I prefer to eject my writing diamonds and rocks into a handwritten journal. I sit down every day, set a timer for a minimum of fifteen minutes, and write non stop. Most of the time I am ejecting rubble onto the page; but occasionally I can see rough writing diamonds scattered among the rocks.

Other people prefer to dictate ideas into a voice recorder, or directly into speech recognition software. Find a way that works for you, and then commit to practicing every day.

*You will find on the next pages the basic guidelines of the Writing Diamonds Journal, which we teach in the Diamond Publishing System™ training modules.*

*They were originally adapted from the methods shared by one of an American writer, Natalie Goldberg in her books, Writing Down the Bones and Wild Mind.*

*These guidelines form the foundation of writing skills that have helped us and thousands of others find their unique voice, and the confidence to write, publish and promote valuable writing diamonds.*

# Writing Diamonds
# Journal Guidelines

1. *Close Out the World.*
   Write in a private space with the door shut.

2. *The Only Limit is Time.*
   Set a timer for a minimum of 15 minutes.

3. *Be a Beginner.*
   Don't worry about making mistakes.

4. *Write Non-Stop.*
   Keep writing as fast as you can, until the timer goes off.

5. *Write Rocks and Nonsense.*
   Anything is better than nothing. Go for it.

6. *Tell It Like It Really Is.*
   There's no one to impress, so just be you.

7. *Pour Everything Out.*
   Let the emotions flow; they make your writing unique.

8.  *Keep Your Rough Writing Diamonds and Rocks to Yourself.*
    This is your private writing diamond pipeline.
    Do <u>not</u> share!

9.  *Always be Prepared to Write.*
    Carry a notebook and pen with you for those unexpected waiting times.

10. *Use a Prompt.*
    Prompts help focus you and get you started.

# Writing Diamonds Stage I Manual & Tools

## Module I: Diamond Writer Manual

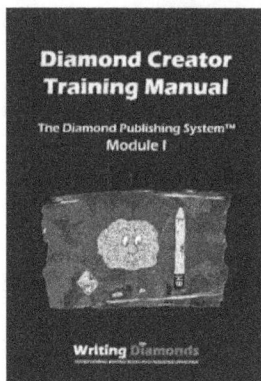

The training manual for *Module I: Diamond Creator* is available to purchase and study at home.

This module focuses on the writing practice process, which helps you to develop new skills, and banish writer's block forever.

Allow four weeks to study the material, and complete the lessons. It is recommended that you purchase the companion *Writing Diamonds Journal and eCourse* to get the most benefit from the lessons.

## Writing Diamonds Journal & eCourse

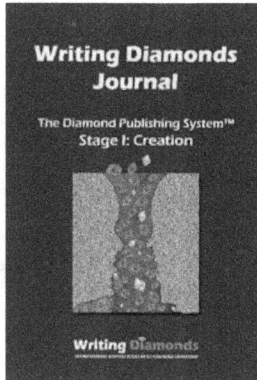

The *Writing Diamonds Journal* is the tool which will help rough writing diamonds to emerge from deep within you.

It can be compared to the process of crystallised carbon being ejected onto the surface of the earth's crust.

The journal also includes the *Daily Writing Prompts eCourse* which is sent to your email inbox. You will receive the journal's writing prompts, as well as bonus insights into the writing practice process.

**The training manual and journal can be purchased from our website.**

# Diamond Explorer

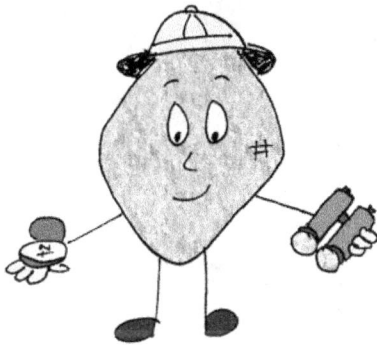

Natural diamonds are discovered by explorers who spend years searching for them. Prospective mines need investors with hundreds of millions of dollars to carry out feasibility studies and fund the set up costs. Writing diamonds are discovered only after you explore the viability of ideas that have emerged from your KESWIN. Stage II takes your best ideas, puts them through a feasibility study, and then creates a plan for your writing project.

## *Stage II: Exploration*

It is essential to explore, study and plan in order for any venture to be successful. Writing and book authoring is no different. We like to approach publishing as if each title is a standalone business investment. This means that it needs to produce a profit, either from sales of the book, or the product or service it is promoting.

For the purpose of this overview, we won't go into details of the business side of book publishing For individuals who want to take this a step further it is provided as in-depth training at the *Diamond Publishing Training Centre*. We will, however, provide some key points for you to think about here.

1. *Write for an Audience.* Before you invest your time and resources into writing and publishing a book, make sure that your topic and content has an interested audience. Do market research first. Test content in a live environment. More on this in the next section.

2. *Develop Feedback Skills.* Learn how to be open to, and accept feedback, because as you write and share your work, you are going to receive plenty of it. Sometimes

this is uninvited, critical and unwelcome. We have a separate eBook: *Critiquing Writing Diamonds: The Art of Receiving and Giving Feedback*. This is available from the Resource Centre on our website.

3. *Understand Intellectual Property Laws.* It is important to protect your Intellectual Property (IP) and Copyright, as much as it is to respect the rights of others. Take time to learn about IP Legislation for your country and what, if any, International Conventions cover you in other regions.

4. *To Outsource or Not to Outsource.* There are plenty of outsourcing options available, but not all are created equal when it comes to writing and publishing. Make sure if you outsource, you do it right. You have invested a lot of time and money in developing your KESWIN; often a third party cannot do this justice.

We would recommend that you do NOT outsource the writing or revision stages. To add the professional polish to your work, consider outsourcing some or all of the following tasks: developmental and copy editing, design, production, proofreading, printing, distribution and marketing. If you do outsource, use local resources. This gives you more control over the project and leaves less room for expensive errors and misunderstandings that may be caused by geographic distance, cultural differences and/or language translations.

If you choose to outsource, do your due diligence. Interview the people you want to work with. Ask them to show you samples of previous work. Contact some of the people who wrote references or testimonials about them. It is important that the freelancers and businesses you work with have the skills and expertise to add value to your project.

When you do sign up with them, make sure that you communicate your brief, including specific requirements and dead-lines, as well as any changes to them with as much clarity as possible. Give them a mock-up of what you want, or show them examples of other people's work that you like.

*Check out our article How to Prevent Outsourcing Breakages in the Resource Centre on our website.*

# Planning the Content For Your Book

For the purpose of this example, we are planning a 5,000 word length book. While this is quite short for a book, it is a good starting point for a novice self-publisher.

You may have discovered an idea during your writing practice that you feel could be turned into a book. You have checked with your target audience, received feedback and now you are ready to transform your rough writing rock into a published diamond.

Before you begin, you need to sit down and plan. While you could work on this intuitively, it is faster, and less stressful, to create a skeleton frame to flesh out when you write.

## Diamond Writing Planning Tips

1. *Decide Your Call to Action.*

   This is the action you want the reader to take at the end of the book. There is no point to writing a book unless you know the purpose of it. For business owners and industry experts, often it is to add credibility to what you are doing, or to inform, educate and pre-sell to the reader. In all these cases, we're sure you want your reader to take some action at the end of the book. So make this your first decision. For instance, at the end of this book, we want you, the reader, to start writing your book.

2. *Provide Key Information.*

   This is the information or key points that will help the reader make their decision about whether they will answer your call to action. For a 5,000 word eBook, 3-4 key points will be sufficient. These key points will make up chapters. As a business owner or industry expert, you may already have something, such as articles or blog posts, which you can repurpose into a book. For example, this book is designed to be an overview of *The Diamond Publishing System™*. As we have spent time developing training modules and other related material, it has made it quite easy for us to break this book into chapters based on those training modules.

3. *Write the Introduction Last.*

This seems crazy, we know, but it is usually why most novice writers fail. They sit down to write a book in a linear order, then get stuck at the beginning because they haven't thought about the first two steps we've outlined above. So they sit staring at the screen, scratching their head, and wondering what their book is going to be about.

The best advice we can give you is the same as you'll receive for any other project. When you make plans you begin with the end goal in mind, and then work backwards. Writing a book is no different. Get clear on the end result, then the topics, and then you will be able to easily write the introduction for them.

## Your Skeleton Frame

Now you will have a skeleton for your book that looks something like this:

1. Introduction
2. Chapter One (Key Point One)
3. Chapter Two (Key Point Two)
4. Chapter Three (Key Point Three)
5. Chapter Four (Key Point Four)
6. Conclusion (Call to Action)

This allows you to take your proposed final word count and divide it by the number of sections, to give you a rough idea of how long each section should be. If we divide our example of 5,000 words by six, we'll aim for approximately 833 words per section. However, we'd recommend you make each chapter around 1,000 words and leave the introduction and conclusion at around 500 words each.

When you have your outline completed, you will be ready to move onto the next stage of the *Diamond Publishing System™: Diamond Writer*.

# Diamond Writer

Natural diamonds are mined from primary (kimberlite pipes) and secondary (river bed and ocean floor) deposit areas. This is a very labour intensive process, which requires miners to sift through tonnes of rocks, ice, dirt and sand, then sort the rough diamonds into grades. Stage III mines the writing diamonds from your journal, your KESWIN, and research sources. Stage IV grades them into articles, blog posts, reports, and book-length manuscripts.

## *Stage III: Mining*

The mining stage for a Diamond Writer is the research and first proper draft stage of the project. You are searching your primary deposit areas (your journals and KESWIN) for rough writing diamonds that can be cut and polished into valuable content. You are also accessing secondary deposit areas such as libraries, the Internet and other resources to add value from third parties to your own KESWIN.

In general, business owners and industry experts already have enough KESWIN that any required mining is not too labour intensive. This is great, because it means that they can begin fleshing out the skeleton they put together during the planning stage without too many distractions.

The less distractions you have, the better. If you are continually stopping and starting to refer to notes, or third party content, then this will show in your work.

The best advice for a novice writer is to have confidence and trust in your KESWIN. Make this a closed book exercise. Lock the door on the external world (even the Internet) for 90 minute periods. The less you refer to external resources (even your writing practice journals), the less risk you have of violating someone else's copyright.

Type (or dictate) your thoughts into a text editor, fleshing out each point of the skeleton outline with information from your journal or research notes.

If you do write anything down, and feel it is not original or needs verifying, make a note in bold and in brackets as you write. This will help you to remember to check it later on in the cutting and polishing stages.

## *Stage IV: Grading*

You can test your work by publishing each key point as a newsletter, article, or blog post. Ask your database, network, social media followers or readers to give you feedback. You will find this helps you fine tune your material to what your audience is really interested in or needs to know.

When you share your work in this way, you will need to specify the feedback you are looking for, either at the start, or invite them to discuss the content at the end. This is also a great way to engage your audience, increase your authority in your industry, and even build existing or new relationships with your database and network. Essentially what you are doing here is making sure you are writing what people want to read, and also grooming them to pre-order your book prior to publication.

Expect to do a lot of revisions. It's the mark of a professional author. By writing shorter pieces, and getting your supporters to grade them, you will cut out some of the heartache in the editing stage.

Once you have analysed the results from your test pieces, you can then go back through the manuscript and make your changes. You may even discover new key points or replace ones that weren't quite as important as you thought.

By the end of the Grading stage, you will have rewritten parts or all of your book manuscript at least once. You will be able to clearly see the value in the book you are writing, and be ready to begin the *Editing Stage of the Diamond Publishing System™*.

*'Books aren't written, they are rewritten.
Including your own. It is one of the hardest
things to accept, especially after the seventh
rewrite hasn't quite done it.'*
*Michael Crichton*

# Diamond Editor

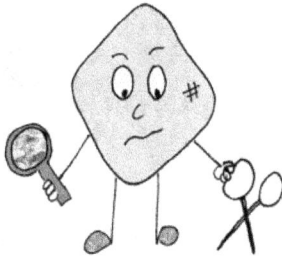

*Natural diamonds are cut and polished in Diamond Cutting Centres. It takes skill and experience to cut a stone to measure up to globally recognised standards of quality. The most visible difference between an ideal cut stone and poorly cut one is the sparkle (or lack of it). Writing diamonds need to be cut and polished into shape so that they sparkle. Stage V professionally cuts the book by taking it through several rounds of editing to improve the writing. Stage VI polishes it by removing the flaws in the spelling, grammar and*

## *Stage V: Cutting*

Although you may have rewritten several parts, or all, of your manuscript by this stage, the work is not over. This is one stage that may be worth handing over to a professional editor, or at the very least, someone who has an excellent eye for detail when it comes to the written word. If not, then we advise you set the project aside for a week or more before you start editing it.

Failing all of those options, print out a hardcopy of your manuscript and work from this.

**Never edit from a computer screen or mobile device.** The reason for this is that your brain is conditioned to scan text on screens, but will read printed text in detail.

Reading from paper is also much easier on your eyes than backlit LCD screens. If you want to pick up as many errors as possible for any piece of writing you make public, then make sure you print it out. This is as relevant for emails, newsletters and online content (including blogs, websites and social media postings), as it is for print and digital publications.

The cutting stage requires fresh eyes and a fresh perspective on your book. It needs to be read from a novice point of view.

Ask: 'What if I knew nothing about this topic and picked up this book to read? How would I find the material? Would it engage me, or would it bore me? Would it help me, or would it confuse me?'

## Flaws to Look For:

- *Jargon or Technical References.*
  These include anagrams, words, technical references and terminology which relate specifically to your industry or topic. Unless you are writing your content for your contemporaries, put everything in simple layman's terms.

- *Anagrams.* Minimise the use of them or avoid them completely, especially if the audience is unfamiliar with them. They are too disruptive to the flow when the reader has to remember what they mean, or needs to keep referring to a glossary.

- *Repetition, Redundancy and Rhetoric.*
  Never belabour a point. Avoid the use of unnecessary words. Don't try to pretty adverbs up with redundant adjectives,
  i.e. "The production costs were horribly expensive."
  Never use double adverbs, i.e. "The experiments were carried out absolutely correctly."
  Keep everything clear, simple and easy to understand.

- *Relevance and Clarity.*
Is your key point in each chapter clear? Does your call to action inspire you to act? Is each sentence relevant to the overall topic?

- *Engagement.* Is the text interesting and relevant? Do the words flow easily? Can you identify your unique voice in your words (or can other readers identify it)? Do you come across as confident, credible and authoritative?

- *Readability.* Only share what the reader needs to know, in simple sentences. Make the text appropriate, informal and personal (you, your, we, I, our). Be direct with what you mean. Use active language (think in terms of doing, not having done or about to do).

- *Images.* If you use any supporting images, do they add value or relevance to the text around them? If not, replace or discard them.

- *Grammar and Punctuation.*
Go through and make sure this is all in order. Do not overuse quote marks, italics, bold, or bullet points. Two of the most common mistakes that amateur writers make are the overuse of quotation marks around words or phrases that don't need them, and exclamation marks. Keep all of these to the bare minimum or remove them completely from the text.

## How to Write with Style

If you are finding it difficult to write with simplicity, clarity and flow, then we would recommend the following two books:

- Elements of Style — E. B. White and William Strunk, Jr.
- On Writing Well — William Zinsser

## The Different Types of Editing

Each editing round will require a different type of editing. This is a brief definition of each:

- *Developmental Editing:* Also referred to as structural or substantive editing. The manuscript goes through one or more rewrites to fix problems such as structure, organisation, coherence and logical consistencies.

- *Line Editing:* Line by line editing to improve clarity, logic and flow.

- *Copyediting:* Improves formatting, style and accuracy.

- *Proofreading:* The galley proofs are read after the book has been designed, laid out and typeset, but before printing or being converted to a digital ebook or pdf file.

## Address Legal Issues

This is also a good time to look for any potential legal time bombs.

- Are all your supporting facts, statistics or quotes correct?

- Do you have permission or licenses to use copyrighted material or intellectual property from third parties?

- Have you referenced third party material appropriately?

- If you are giving health, well-being, legal or financial advice, have you put a disclaimer at the front of the book (even if you are professionally qualified in the area you are giving advice on)?

- Do you need a lawyer to read through your manuscript to make sure it is free of any copyright, libel, illegal reproduction, privacy invasion, or negligence issues?

*If you have any doubts about some of your content, leave it out.*

## *Stage VI: Polishing*

When you feel you have rewritten, cut and verified all your material and produced the manuscript to the best of your ability, you need to polish it before you move to the production stage.

Use a professional editing service rather than rely on your own skills, or that of volunteers such as friends, family or other willing supporters.

Using volunteer editors or proofreaders, while free, can come with hidden costs. Yes, it is great to get their support and assistance with this, and other steps of the project. However, because they are giving their time voluntarily, it is their time, and time is money. So generally they will rush through the text and miss mistakes, or they may not pick up on any possible legal issues. Mistakes could cost you later on to get a professional to fix. It could also damage your reputation or worse, you could end up paying a lawyer to defend you in court.

If you decide to polish the material yourself, leave it for a few days, or better still weeks before reviewing it. You could also run it through proofreading software, such as Grammarly.com. This picks up spelling, grammar and punctuation errors that inbuilt tools in word processing systems like Microsoft® Word often miss. Grammarly also checks for any plagiarism violations.

One caveat: Grammarly was originally designed for academic assignments, so you need to use your own judgement about its recommendations. On the whole though, this is a really good tool if your spelling and grammar skills are weak, and you don't want to pay for professional editing of your work.

## One Final Polish

Once you are completely satisfied that your manuscript is ready for publishing, print out another hard copy. Again you may need to leave this a few days or weeks to view it with fresh eyes, or ask someone with excellent copyediting and proofreading skills to read it for you.

Carefully go through the hard copy word by word, looking for any flaws you may have missed. We want to ensure that this writing diamond has been cut and polished to perfection (or as close as you can get) before you move onto the *Setting Stage of the Diamond Publishing System™*.

# Diamond Publisher

*After cutting and polishing, natural diamonds are set into precious metal to be sold to jewellery retailers and the end customer. This is done by professionals who have experience in jewellery design and manufacture. Stage VIII takes your publishing ready writing diamonds to production, cover and interior book design, typesetting and layout, printing or digital ebook file conversion, and complying with legal deposit laws.*

## *Stage VII: Setting*

Once you have polished your manuscript to perfectly formed brilliance, you will need to set it into book format. If you haven't already designed a cover, do so now. Some people like to design the cover first, to give them incentive to write the book. However, we recommend waiting until you really get to know the book's content, which also makes it easier to write the back cover sales copy.

You will also add the front and end matter, contents and index, apply for an ISBN number, and start announcing its release date to the world.

## Do You Need an ISBN?

ISBN stands for International Standard Book Number. It is the basic identifier of the book, and one ISBN is issued for each format of the book being published.

We recommend that you apply for your own ISBNs, rather than get one through a publishing service.

In some countries, such as New Zealand and Canada, they are issued free from the national library. In other countries they are sold through a central agency, with the cost reducing per ISBN as the purchase quantity increases.

Even if you have to pay for ISBNs, it is worth the investment, as it adds your book to the national catalogue, and will increase the chances of sales to libraries, educational institutions and even retail bookstores.

It also makes it uniquely identifiable in international searches, and helps the book industry determine the publishing country and sales statistics.

## Book Title

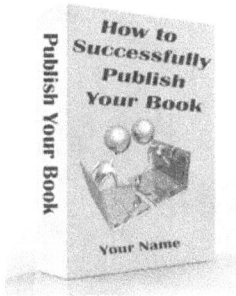

You may have been working with what you think is a great title, but is it?

It is extremely important to give your book the best title you can. So take the time to put some serious thought into one.

Do some brainstorming alone, with trusted team members and other advisors. Google your possible titles to make sure they haven't already been used. You can change this title right up to the moment you finalise your cover design.

A client asked us about using a swear word in their title (along the lines of *"when the s\*\*\* hits the fan"*). We would recommend you use your judgement on this. First, ask yourself if using it is in line with your branding, and if it would impact negatively or positively on your professionalism and expertise. If you still want to use it, then do a Google AND Amazon search to see if the relevant word has been used in other reputable books.

## Cover and Interior Design

The cover design and interior of a book can make or break the success of your project. If you want to come across as a professional and credible expert on your topic, it pays to invest in professional design.

When you hire a book designer, ask to see samples of their work. You don't want to waste your money by hiring the wrong person. Make sure they have worked on non-fiction books, as the process for designing and laying out a novel is quite different to a reference or non-fiction book. Get samples of work they have done.

If you hope to get your book into retail stores, then it must have a professional finish to it. Buyers make their decisions after a quick flick through your book.

One of the things we love about book publishing is that you can release your book in different formats. However, be aware that digital formats require a different layout and file conversion than a printed publication, so this could add to any outsourcing expense.

If you choose to do the design and laying out yourself, we advise that you invest in design software. This will give your book a far more professional finish that Microsoft® Word can. We have tested a few design programmes. Serif PagePlus™ has been the best so far for simplicity, intuitiveness and value for money.

## *The Different Book Formats*

In today's world, books come in different formats, which we'll look at in this section, as well as discuss the advantages and disadvantages of each.

## Print Books

Print books are ideal for non-fiction books that share your KESWIN. They are a tangible product for you to sell in your business or at live events, and look more impressive than a stack of discs.

Remember that sales are all about getting the customer to say "Yes!" now, while they are standing in front of you. If you hand them a flyer with a link to your digital book for sale on the Internet, it is quite likely they will never follow up. The most common reason for this is they get distracted with other things. The moment they leave your side, your

Deb Donnell

book fades from their memory, as does their desire to support you.

We love to buy non-fiction books in print format because it is easy to flick through them to find information at a later date.

We also feel that the information is more credible than in digital format, because the author and publisher believes enough in the title to make the financial commitment of print production.

If you choose to print your book, we would advise the following:

1. *Print locally.* Find a local printer who prints books on a regular basis. Usually they will have someone on their team who can provide you with guidance and input into your project. We have been extremely blessed with the publishing expert at our local printer. He has 40 plus years' experience in the publishing industry. He adds value to our ventures, and reaffirms our KESWIN.

One of the main reasons we choose to print locally, and also use local suppliers wherever we can, is that we are helping support our local economy. Our city was devastated by earthquakes in 2010 and 2011. Many of our businesses were severely impacted, which had a flow on effect to the employment market and our economy. In our opinion it makes economic sense to spend and invest our money locally, rather than disperse it overseas.

Economic recession has impacted all over the world in recent years. One of the causes is that people sacrifice quality and craftsmanship for price. However the lower price goods are often manufactured overseas where labour is cheap. The lower quality of the finished product also reflects this. The cheap mentality is now expanding into services, with the many providers choosing to take advantage of modern technology and outsource to India or Asia.

Unfortunately this has had a damaging effect on local economies. We would urge you to think hard about who you are choosing to supply your goods and services. Ask yourself if the benefits really do outweigh the negatives, and what is the real impact of where you are spending your money?

2. *Use quality paper and cover laminates.*
Another reason for printing locally is you get to see paper stock samples and other work the printer has done. This way you can ensure that the paper you use for the interior and cover is of a professional standard. Many books printed overseas use low grade paper, unless you pay extra to upgrade to trade standard paper quality. The

cost of the upgrade often increases the price per book to more than if you'd printed locally.

3. *Get the galley proofs or a cast off copy of the book, before you approve the print-run.*
This gives you control over the print and image quality, as well as the chance to address any file conversion issues before the full print-run begins. [Note: Any changes at this stage could be expensive.] You rarely get proofs or cast-offs when when you are working with an overseas printer. In my opinion, getting the galley proofs is one of the most exciting stages of book publishing.

4. *Ask to see the book on the printing press.*
This is another exciting moment in book publishing, and well worth building a good relationship with your local print team.

5. *Keep the print runs small.*
Start off with 50-100 copies to make the project affordable.

6. *Set up a trade account with your printer.*
This is one reason why we choose to print locally. If we printed overseas we'd have to pay for the books when we placed the order. By the time you add in freight from overseas and any bank service or finance charges, the cost of printing ends up being comparable or higher. Our

local printer extends us credit to 20th of the month following, which means we can often cover the account with income from sales before payment is due.

## Negatives to Printing Books

There aren't too many, apart from you may have unsold stock to store. Avoid this by printing in smaller quantities. Studies show that the average sales quantity for non-fiction books is less than 250 copies. Make this your maximum print run. It may be best to start off with getting 50 or 100 copies printed, and then print again when you sell out, rather than store unsold stock.

Another negative is shipping overseas can be as much as, or more than the book is selling for. As this is at the customer's cost, it may deter international sales.

If you use an overseas printer, make sure they are reputable and trustworthy. The last thing you want is to find your content stolen and repackaged under another title and author's name.

## Print-on-Demand Books

There are companies who will print books on demand for authors. This means that when a customer makes an order, they have the freedom to choose the format, and a single copy of the book is printed and shipped. Lulu, Xlibris, Self-Express and Create Space (Amazon) are examples of Print on Demand companies.

The author is responsible for the writing and publishing process. Be aware that even though you do get to choose the price of your book and your royalty (or profit), the print on demand company has the right to offer discounts to their readers whenever they want. This means that your royalty may not always be the amount that you anticipated.

Payment will not be immediate, and it could take several months before you see any income from your hard work.

You, as the author and publisher, are still responsible for marketing your titles and your book's sales success will depend on this.

In our opinion, the biggest negative is that the Print on Demand company is building their database from their client's hard work. This is known as Digital Sharecropping.

It means that you'll never know who has bought your book, and therefore you'll never be able to market directly to them.

However, there are benefits to the Print on Demand option during the production stage of your soft cover book due to the low cost of single copies or small quantity print runs.

We often will upload our files and order a proof copy to see how the book will look in its finished form. This can work out cheaper than ordering one copy only of your book from your local printer.

You may be planning to send out prepublication review copies to get some testimonials to put in your book before it's released onto the market. If you want to give your reviewers a fully bound copy, rather than galley proofs, then a handful of copies from a print on demand company may be an option to consider.

## Digital Books

Technology has made it very easy and affordable for people to independently or self-publish (this is often referred to as indie publishing). Unfortunately a large number of self-published books are released without having been properly edited (if at all), or designed to a professional standard.

There are different digital formats which are discussed as follows:

## eBooks

eBooks are published in a format that can only be read on an eBook reader, or with an eBook reading app. The file extension will depend of the platform. Examples are .epub, .mobi, .html and of course the proprietary formats for Amazon Kindle and iBooks. You may need to purchase additional software (such as Serif PagePlus™) to convert your original file to these formats.

Some of the readers, such as the Kindle e-Ink readers, only display books in greyscale (16 shades). This is because they are designed specifically for text display. While we won't get into the technical side of e-Ink screens versus backlit LCD screens here, remember that the latter is multi-purpose and designed to display full colour graphic images and videos. If your book includes a lot of colour images, then you need to be aware that some readers won't get the full value of your content.

eBook content is fluid. It allows the reader to choose their preferred text size and font style (i.e. serif and sans-serif). Images will move with the fluid text. So if your book contains a lot of images, with captions, this could become a distraction for the reader. It also makes quality control challenging. If you are producing an image heavy book for overseas customers, we would recommend that you consider print on demand rather than eBook format.

Like print on demand books, eBooks are usually sold through eBook distribution companies such as Xlibris, Smashwords™, Amazon-Kindle, iTunes, etc. As with print on demand books, you get to control the publishing process, set the royalty amount and even make updates to your book over time.

However, it is important to be aware of the negatives, which are the same as discussed in the print on demand section. You don't have a say in your book being offered at a discount, which impacts upon your royalty payment. Payment can take months to arrive, and could be subject to foreign currency conversion bank charges. You do not know who your customer is. You are working hard to write and produce your book, then subject yourself to the perils of digital sharecropping. If you do make an update, you have to write to their support team, and make a plea for them to advise their customer (your reader).

Some eBook distributors don't sell the book, they just lease it to their customers. This gives them the right to delete your book from their customer's device.

You also get no control of reader reviews. Some companies seem to attract trolls who take great pleasure in writing bad reviews. Activity like this could damage your brand and may even destroy your business.

You are competing against millions of titles in the bigger companies. If you're going to work hard marketing your book, you may as well direct people to your site to buy from, rather than someone else's.

The advantages to having a digital format book means that there are no shipping costs and therefore you can sell your book easier overseas. Your audience is bigger. You can also set your book up in Microsoft® Word and other text or publishing software like Serif PagePlus™.

*Check out our eBook 6 Rock Solid Elements to EBook Publishing in our Resource Centre.*

## Sales Trends 2015

*The latest statistics by the Association of American Publishers shows that e-book sales are down by 7.5% for the first quarter of 2015. Trade paperback sales appear to be making a comeback, with sales up 8.5%.*

*This trend of people switching back to paper-back is also repeated in other regions, not just the US.*

There could be several reasons for this:

- Sales are measured through ISBNs, and many self-published books don't have ISBNs.

- Print books carry a true sense of ownership, and the mass market are starting to realise this.

- The novelty of eBooks/eReaders is passing.

- eBooks are more suited to niche markets, rather than the mass market.

We do believe that it is best to publish your book in several formats, which gives your customer choices, and therefore an increase in sales for you.

CREATING PUBLISHED DIAMONDS

*We follow the industry trends and send a regular summary report to people on our database. If you're not on our list, please to go our website and submit your details in the form on our about page.*

## PDF eBooks

PDF ebooks are very easy to produce — almost too easy. After all, Microsoft® Office software allows you to save your files as pdfs. But how secure are they?

If you are concerned about security of your Intellectual Property (and you should be), then I would recommend you invest in pdf conversion software that makes the file fully secure. This is another advantage of Serif PagePlus™. You can even choose an option when you save the file that prevents your reader printing out the pdf or eBook from their computer.

The beauty of publishing in pdf format is that your readers don't need apps or eBook reader platforms to read them. You can sell the book direct from your own website or via emails and newsletters to your database. Avoid uploading pdf files to your social and online network sites. Many, like Facebook and Google, state in their terms and conditions that you waive exclusive rights to any content you upload. You've worked hard to develop your Intellectual Property, so do your best to avoid being the victim of digital sharecropping.

## What is Digital Sharecropping?

**Digital Sharecropping** is a term first coined by Nicolas Carr in 2006. It is a great way to describe how dangerous it is to put your Intellectual Property and hard work into the hands of others.

Reference www.roughtype.com/?p=634

People (the sharecroppers) choose the free options available on the Internet to post their digital content, for self-expression or socialising purposes. They're not interested in making money — in fact, they believe that the economic value of their content is trivial. Their goal is to connect with others, and get some attention from them.

However the digital landlords or overseers are reaping the economic rewards from their sharecroppers' efforts. They are getting traffic to their online real estate investment, and then leveraging off their sharecroppers' free-labour to make money.

To give you an example — let's look closely at Facebook.

- It is a collection of User Profiles and Business Pages = 1.49 billion active users (as at the second quarter of 2015). Active Users are people who have logged in during the last 30 days.

- Each user has signed up to Facebook's terms and conditions, which includes giving Facebook full licensing rights to use any content they upload to their profile, or page.

- They have also given Facebook permission to market to them, which Facebook now does with sponsored (paid) advertising.

- Facebook's terms and conditions also allow Facebook to change the rules at any time, including how content is shared to its traffic.

- And if you are deemed to have violated Facebook's terms and conditions your business page, user profile, etc will be deleted.

## Legal Deposit Obligations

When you publish a book, you will need to comply with the publishing legislation specific to your country.

This may include copyright filing, and sending archive copies to a legal deposit with your national library.

For details specific to your country, please do an online search by entering your country's name along with keywords "Book Legal Deposit" into your preferred Internet search engine.

# Diamond Marketer

    *Diamonds and diamond set jewellery are marketed and sold through a variety of channels online and offline. Stage VIII shows you how to promote and sell your published diamonds through several channels online and offline.*

## *Stage VIII: Promotion*

Regardless of the setting and sales and distribution channels you choose for your book, the sales success depends on how well you promote it. We recommend that you plan out a campaign with the focus mainly on no or low cost marketing methods. Dedicate a minimum of three years to each title you love. You need to spend time every day promoting your book. Some of your efforts will work, while others will feel like a futile exercise.

Unfortunately marketing online is as challenging, if not more challenging, as it is offline. Pursue as many inbound marketing avenues as possible. Some things to consider:

1. *Decide on your book's official release date.* Advise everyone you can think of about it. Hold a book launch party to celebrate your achievement and make some sales.

2. *Send out media releases.* You are more likely to have success with local media rather than national or international. Establish, nurture and grow any media contacts. Offer to be interviewed. Create a human interest angle if you can.

3. *Generate quality reviews.* Don't be afraid to send out review copies to book reviewers, industry leaders and even well respected public figures.

4. *Develop public speaking skills.* Offer to speak to groups and at events relevant to your topic. Be willing to do this for free, on the condition that you are allowed to set up a sales table for your books.

5. *Tell people you have written a book.* Talk about it to them (just do not become a bore about your baby). Your promotion should be conversational. Do ask for the sale but do not push if they say no.

6. *Build your networks and your database.* The money really is in the list, and so this is where your most success lies. This is the reason why we urge caution at distributing your books through digital sharecropping companies.

John Kremer's book *1001 Ways to Market Your Book* is a great resource. Just don't get overwhelmed with ideas. Pick two or three you feel comfortable with, and implement them. Measure results; don't spend too long on a technique that isn't creating sales.

## Raising Your Best Seller

A lot of published authors compare the publishing process to pregnancy and birth, but with a much longer gestation period (sometimes years instead of months).

Viewing your book as if it is a helpless child is a good idea, because it needs your full commitment to ensure its success. After all, you've worked hard to write and publish it, so please don't give up on it now.

When you write your marketing plan, define what 'best seller' really means to you. Is it to sell out the print run? To make a profit? To sell more books than a previous title you've published (or your competitor has).

Do not get hung up on the official best seller lists. They are based on sales through the retail market of ISBN issued titles over a period of a week. It doesn't record direct sales figures (publisher/author to reader). There's also no magic number to aim for, as there are slow weeks, and peak selling weeks. Often a title's weekly sales needs to be in the tens of thousands to hit the lists.

Some best seller lists get manipulated by the publisher or author who has deep pockets (such as a spare $100,000 to $200,000 lying around). They will use a service that bulk buys books from retailers, but makes them look like organic sales.

Other titles become best sellers because the author has given away a huge number of books to people and asked them to create buzz about the book through rave reviews and viral marketing methods.

And then there's the overnight best seller which never is overnight, and may be better termed as a sleeper that has just been woken up. The author has slogged their guts out and persevered against all odds to become an 'overnight' success.

*To learn more please refer to the eBook How to Raise a Best Seller in our Resource Centre.*

## Release Your Book

We hope that this overview of the *Diamond Publishing System™* has inspired you to start working on your book. Like the formation, mining and manufacturing of natural diamonds, it does take hard work to transform your writing rocks into published diamonds. However, the process is made a lot easier by following a proven system.

It is also much more enjoyable when you work in a safe, nurturing and supportive environment such as the *Writing Diamonds Training Centre.*

# Writing Diamonds
## Training Centre
Content Writing and Book Publishing

We provide training, mentoring and consulting to people who want to transform writing rocks into published diamonds. The *Diamond Publishing System™* is delivered in six training modules, with assignments focusing on the research, writing, editing, publishing and marketing of *your* book.

As a member of the *Writing Diamonds Training Centre* you will proceed from first idea to final sale with experienced guides to help you. It is possible to complete the training modules and release your first book within eight months. This will, of course, depend on your level of commitment, your resources and your efforts.

Members also have full access to our Membership Community, News and Articles, Event Centre, Webinars and Workshops, Resource Library and Diamond Bourse. The Diamond Bourse is our trading centre where you can buy discounted products and services from approved suppliers, as well as the books published by our graduates.

There are three levels of membership; choose the one that best matches your learning style and your publishing goals.

## SI-Membership

This is great for self-driven learners, who want to retain independence and control of their project, but would also like the support of a network of like minded people. Membership is limited, which keeps the environment positive and nurturing. Members have full access to the resources and community in the secure online training centre.

## VS-Membership

These are group workshops offered online (and offline by arrangement). Groups are limited to a maximum of 20 people, and are delivered as six modules, over 4-8 weeks each in length. Members work on their own book project, but have the support and strength of their peers and trainers in a group environment, as well as full access to the online training centre.

## IF-Membership

For people who prefer private coaching. This is tailored to the individual's needs and their project. The IF Member meets with their assigned coach for a 90 minute weekly session, via Skype, or in person where possible. They also have full access to the online training centre. This option is subject to availability, and application approval.

## *Also Available from Writing Diamonds Ltd*

### Add-on Publishing and Consulting Services

We can also help with all aspects of writing and publishing, including project management, editing, design production, distribution and marketing. This is charged on a per service or per project basis.

### Home Study Manuals, Workbooks and eCourses

This is ideal for people who want to learn the *Diamond Publishing System*™ but would prefer not to join the online training centre. These are available for purchase in digital and print formats from our website.

### *The Next Step*

To join our training centre, or purchase any of our services or products, please contact us through one of the methods listed on the last page of this book.

# Testimonials

'Writing Diamonds provides a fresh approach to learning online. The mentors and members are real people you can talk to and build lasting relationships with. The training is professional and easy to follow. The workshops are fun and interactive. You can get your questions answered immediately, which is especially valuable when you have a problem you can't work out on your own.'
— Corinne Floyd, Canada (VS Member)

'Working with Writing Diamonds gave me a real understanding of the factors involved to publish a book. I never would have completed my project without their help.'
— David Clarkson, New Zealand (IF Member)

'Writing Diamonds has made me really excited about writing. I just needed someone to get me in the habit and doing it. Now I feel I am on a roll. The presentation on writing our 'about me' page was outstanding and helped me so much.'
— Nicole Thomas, USA (VS Member)

'It's awesome having Writing Diamonds work with me to produce a real book. They deliver clear instructions and give practical support in a friendly and approachable manner.'
— Dr Alan Fayter, New Zealand (IF Member)

'I have written more since Writing Diamonds showed me how to write than at any other time. I do believe that within us all there are diamonds that need to be put down on paper. When they are inside of us, nobody ever sees or hears them. Now that I write every day I feel a sense of who I am and who I might become. And to think I almost didn't take this course. What a loss I would have experienced.'
— Greg Gust, USA (VS Member)

'Writing Diamonds provide good information in their workshops, especially relating to the legal requirements and other aspects of publishing.'
— Jane Cowan-Harris, New Zealand (IF Member)

'Being a member of Writing Diamonds has helped my writing skills improve tremendously. Now, I not only have the confidence to sit and write, but I have the basic ability to communicate intelligibly while delivering some real value. This was a skill that was well beyond me prior to becoming a miner in the Writing Diamonds Training Centre.'
— Tom Renfro, USA (VS Member)

# Recommended Reading, Software and Training

Throughout this book we have mentioned several books and tools to help you with your self-publishing journey. These are available in the Resource Centre on our website: http://WritingDiamonds.com/ResourceCentre

- [EBook] Critiquing Writing Diamonds: The Art of Receiving and Giving Feedback

- [Training Manual] Module 1: Diamond Writer

- [Workbook/eMail Course] Writing Diamonds Journal and Daily Writing Prompts

- [Article] How to Prevent Outsourcing Breakages

- [Print Book] Elements of Style — E. B. White and William Strunk, Jr.

- [Print Book] On Writing Well — William Zinsser

- [Software] Grammarly

- [Software] Serif PagePlus®

- [EBook] Six Rock Solid Elements to eBook Publishing

- [EBook] Diamond Explorer's First Website

- [Print Book] 1001 Ways to Market Your Books — John Kremer

- [EBook] How to Raise a Best Seller

- [Membership Site] Writing Diamonds Training Centre

# About the Author — Deb Donnell

Deb Donnell is a professional editor, proofreader, publisher, professional speaker and a GIA Diamonds Graduate (Gemological Institute of America — Natural Diamonds). She developed a love for writing, editing and publishing at the age of ten, and has worked in the jewellery, banking and publishing industries in New Zealand and the United Kingdom.

She is the founder of Keswin Publishing Limited and Writing Diamonds Limited. She has developed *The Diamond Publishing System*™, and used it to publish books for herself and others. Deb's books include the best selling titles *Responders: the Volunteer New Zealand Response Teams Christchurch Earthquake Deployments* (co-authored with Pete Seager), and the *Christchurch Comparison annual editions*.

Deb lives in Christchurch, New Zealand and is committed to documenting the city's ongoing rebuild from the devastating 2010 and 2011 earthquakes. Her primary mission is to help one million people release their trapped books. Will yours be one of them?

To contact Deb for mentoring, consulting, to speak at your next event, or to share your publishing success story, please contact her through WritingDiamonds.com.

# Contact Writing Diamonds

*What are you waiting for?*
*Start working on releasing your trapped book*
*with the team at Writing Diamonds*

Sign up for membership at
*http://WritingDiamonds.com/Training*

Enquire about our publishing and
consulting services
or purchase our training manuals,
workbooks and ecourses

**Online:** WritingDiamonds.com

**Email:** Training@WritingDiamonds.com

Phone: +64 3 421 7834
Our Office Hours
New Zealand Time Zone
Monday to Friday 9 a.m. - 5 p.m.

www.ingramcontent.com/pod-product-compliance
Lightning Source LLC
Chambersburg PA
CBHW070253290326
41930CB00041B/2511